Tender Flower

of

Heaven

Contents

Acknowledgements

Thank you
to all my dear friends
for lending their support and encouragement
and their computer, editing, and artistic skills.
I also thank my family for
their love, support, and flexibility.

Cover Design: Rosalie van den Bos

Cover Photograph: Nature Divine Photography

Dedicated to

Pure Silence

Brahm

The Light of God

The Kingdom of Heaven Within

The Lively Blissful Unified Field of Natural Law

Atman

Our Own Transcendental Self.

Yato vacho nivartante tad dhama paramam mama
From where speech returns
that is my transcendental abode.

Tender Flower of Heaven

Holland, January 1998

The first moment I met you—
        my stillness—
I experienced a certainty—
        a fullness
that I never knew before;
        a peaceful rest
in softness of my Self
        that compressed
life's purpose into this moment
        and impressed
on me life's true meaning.
        I was blessed
with the purest love that exists
        and repossessed
a confidence of knowing—
        knowingness—
that now cushions my life
        in sweetness
allowing me to move free
        unoppressed
in the calm of my Being.
        I confess
I want to sing aloud
        and address
all to experience their silence

and repossess
the beauty of life, of living—
the gentleness
of the tender flower of Heaven.

My Heaven

Holland, July 2006

If I could create my own heaven,
how would I like it to be?
I'd make it just as it is now—
the heaven that exists inside me.

It's a perfect place of ancient silence
that begins to percolate in bubbling bliss,
then opens into soothing waves—
the rising sea falling in stillness.

My heaven is filled with shimmering light
that hums within me as silence's song,
and blissfully pulsates in my physiology
illuminating every cell like the golden dawn.

Rivers of nectar flow from my heart.
I delight in its sweet taste.
It is purest love that exists
in which all life is interlaced.

Here tendrils of my feelings extend to infinity
embracing the entire universe
and pour to God in deepest gratitude
for this gift—my beloved Heaven on Earth.

Inner Geometry

Maharishi Vedic City, January 2008

When I closed my eyes one sweet night,
To my surprise I saw structures of light.
From a point they started to appear—
All conjoined they became increasingly clear.
I saw cylinders, triangles, cones, and figure-eights
In a sky star-spangled, yet silent state.
I saw them transform into one another;
I saw one being born, then the next uncovered.

A few nights later when drifting to sleep
The day's events faded, I felt warm in God's keep.
Into my silence, gently I slid
Suddenly in alliance with a pulsating grid.
A circle within a square I saw in this vision
As if hanging in air with perfect precision.
This matrix of horizontal and vertical lines
Was transfixed yet fluctuated beyond space and time.

Deep in transcendence often I witness
Waves of light form circles of bliss.
Becoming smaller and smaller, they dissolve into Unity,
Then emerge again from point to infinity.
Back and forth they expand and contract
While my stillness remains geometrically intact.
Upon this mirrored silence of pure abstraction
All these forms appear as just a reflection.

In the darkness many nights I see
Vibrating white points open into frequencies.
They pulsate, then begin to unwind
Stretching out into one straight line.
Deep inside I clearly cognize
Mathematical structures of all shapes and size.
Now I know from where geometry begins—
It flows out from a point of my silence within.

Ocean Depths

Maharishi Vedic City, February 2007

Sinking to the bottom of the ocean
my silence sees silence in motion
as gentle waves that rise and fall
washing over me like a warm waterfall.

All around me are effervescent jewels—
thousands of sparkling bubbles forming whirlpools
that draw me into their minutest core
anchoring me deeper to the ocean's floor.

Here I sit, breathless—motionless
in a state of pure blessedness.
The deeper into this silence I succumb
the more I hear silence's hum.

It hums like waves rolling on the shore;
it hums as waves rising that endlessly soar.
Here silence and sound are one continuum
where silence and flow together I become.

Rise, fall, rise, fall—I delight in their swing—
the delicacy of the song the ocean sings.
It sings its own tender flowing dance
moving in ripples that create resonance.

From this still point I see life's totality
the silence, the bubble, the wave, the sea.
In the ocean's depths I have touched my soul;
I have touched my bliss, freeing it to become blissful.

Poetic Flight

Holland, June 2006

The page is staring at me—
blank, lifeless, and white—
waiting for my thoughts to fly free
and my pen to take poetic flight.

I see before me all possibilities—
the bubbling of pure delight.
Silence is unlocking its mysteries
like stars clustering in the night.

The direction is not yet clear
but do I need to know the way?
At this stage I should not fear
for silence over me has sway;

always guiding me from its empty sphere,
its eternal inward play.
My tender feelings I need to hear
as they begin to unfold like a golden ray.

Silence sings its own song
from its ancient flowing hum.
Here the poet's mind belongs
from where the stirring of sound comes.

His words will then burst like the dawn
filling the page with gentle rhythms
and meanings that leap like a fawn
from one's heart into silence's hymns.

Life's Flow

Holland, June 2006

Many roads were before me
but I did not have to choose
as the river holds the deepest clues.
I let life's river carry me
that will reveal true destiny.

Fortunately this river ran fast
taking me in clear, smooth direction
fulfilling my desire of lifetimes past
to know man's perfection
that only inside one can catch.

All powerful is the river's stream
if one can capture its effortless flow;
traversing silently unseen
to an inward glow
where light of Self is redeemed.

Invisible Love

Heavenly Mountain, April 2004

I feel love wherever I go.
My every breath it sustains.
I can't see it, but feel its flow
Like the winds humming refrains.

Its strength supports my every move
Lifting me to cross over the sea.
Its tenderness always soothes
My heart to be happy and free.

As I walk down a lonely road
Love's whispers rustle in the leaves.
I lift my eyes to behold
Its light dancing in the trees.

Love's invisible presence by my side
Is always there to hold my hand,
To guide me in an effortless glide
Inward to Heaven's golden land.

Netted Together in the Underground

Heavenly Mountain, April 2003

Netted together in the underground
all beautiful flowers, plants, and trees—
their roots mingling everywhere—are bound
by this earth, even beneath the sea.

In the underground life is forever born—
here the mechanics of creation lie
where rhythms and cycles of Nature form—
stars, moons, and galaxies in the sky.

Hidden, unseen are Nature's powers
in a field that sings its own song—
a song that hums as soft showers
giving rise to the sun's golden dawn.

Netted together in the underground—
a mosaic tapestry of all men and race.
In each thread of this cloth are found
strands of light weaving God's Grace.

All life is spun in this cosmic web
of silky, soft-textured silence.
Still, yet vibrant, together it weds
man and Nature in alliance.

God is the universal, unseen net
whose golden fabric spreads everywhere.
Here everything is wisely and perfectly set—
in silence we are wrapped in his care.

Love's Sacred Key
Heavenly Mountain, April 2003

Can love be this true, this real?
Every moment the sun is shining.
             My heart is singing
the inner warmth and beauty I feel.

Love's secret has opened to me.
Every moment I am flying high.
             I freely dance
in the discovery of love's sacred key.

The whispers of love so soft and fair
every moment I hear in the wind;
             I hear them also in the brook
as this love follows me here, there, everywhere.

How sweet and tender is this love inside!
Every moment it lifts me to Heaven;
             it fills me to overflowing.
In deep silence this love abides.

Fourth through Seventh States of Consciousness

Heavenly Mountain, April 2003

Stepping into my fourth dimension
all perception melts before me.
Like the canvas of an abstract painting
all forms and colors are fading
into a soft, silent sea.

Stepping into my fifth dimension
I feel outside looking in
to the ever-changing times
of the world that seems out of rhyme
with my silence that flows within.

Stepping into my sixth dimension
life takes on a transparent glow.
A divine texture glorifies my sight
dancing like golden sunlight
sparkling on freshly fallen snow.

Stepping into my seventh dimension
my silence penetrates through life's layers—
through my senses in all directions.
Everything is my Self's inner perfection
singing Self's beauty everywhere.

Spring

Heavenly Mountain, February 2003

Spring is circling round again
as the sun greets me around the bend.
The birds thrill the mountain air
as their echoes reverberate everywhere.

All delight in the budding of spring
in delicate flowers blossoming—
the rose, the jasmine that fill the air
spreading their sweetness everywhere.

In spring each moment is born anew
as new leaves appear in sparkling dew.
New life allows new hope to shine—
hope for peace for all mankind.

If man could walk through spring's gate
he'd rise above his narrow hate
and walking on the fresh-born grass
he'd be renewed in a beauty unsurpassed.

Fairyland

Heavenly Mountain, February 2003

Divine, enchanted fairyland
sparkling in the dawning sun.
Your crystal-covered bejeweled trees
glitter golden for everyone.

Looking closely, you will see
fairies dancing in the sky
as snowflakes fluttering off trees
or diamonds softly floating by.

Silent snow in rainbow hues
creates magic outside my window—
mountain ridges of misty blue—
an ice-land where peace always glows.

To Explore Space

Heavenly Mountain, February 2003

To explore space
     is a quest to know the infinite
to smile with the stars upon the world—
               a minute speck
where differences of all race
     sweetly disappear.

To explore space
     is to go beyond triviality
to transcend the grip of war and hate—
               its futility
compared to Heaven's grace
     that dispels all fear.

To explore space
     is to float free from gravity
while held together by the force of weightlessness
               in the cavity
of a sparkling place
     that inwardly appears.

To explore space
     is to know that outer and inner are one—
man and cosmos—a unified field

where the sun
        shines its golden face
every day each year.

Blue Ridge Mountains

Heavenly Mountain, October 2001

Royal mountains gracing the sky—
a mighty fortress surrounding me.
Behind your shield I safely lie—
guardians, guarding my liberty.

Your walls nothing can penetrate
as to the Heavens you tower.
Invincible is your regal state;
peace is your silent power.

Within your walls one breathes
a soft air of purest sanctity
that spreads around in the breeze
with humming whispers of serenity.

Glorious sun, every day and night
you crown these peaks with golden rays
along with the full moon's chiffon light.
May all the world know this peace, I pray.

Peace Begins Within

Heavenly Mountain, October 2001

Enjoy the beauty that is around you
and see the peace of God's grace
sparkling in summer's breezy hues,
in winter's falling snow-like lace,
in spring's silvery new-born leaves,
in millions of shimmering stars in space,
in the sunrise lighting the morning dew.

Peace sparkles in every grain of sand,
in crimson dropping leaves of fall,
in the moonbeams' pearl-like strands,
in the cooing doves' gentle call,
in mountains towering to the sky,
in graceful birds that flutter by,
in hummingbirds which on petals land.

God's peace begins within
when mind turns inward its eye
and sees the vast, calming ocean
and the stillness of misty, soft sky.
A peaceful heart has the golden key
to sail through life unfettered—free
loving all men as one's own kin.

Peace from the Level of Peace

Heavenly Mountain, October 2001

Every person in every land
is made by God's same hands.
We are one family under one sun
sharing one earth and its oceans.
On the surface we are diverse.
At our depths lies one universe
of consciousness—man's deepest source—
one Unified Field—Nature's unifying force.
Like pearls strung together on a string
our consciousness unifies everything.
Like petals bound to the flower's sap
consciousness—holy waters—every man must tap.
Man must drink from his silent ocean
and be filled with love's emotions
and let waves of peace spread everywhere
bringing peace to the world and love's care.
Knowing peace at the level of peace
is the only way for God's light to increase.

Star Children
Heavenly Mountain, July 2001

We are star-children
      born of supernova stars;
inside are our stellar births
      forming nebulas endlessly far.

We are moon-children
      sliding down moonbeams
whose force controls the tides
      whose light lights our dreams.

We are sun-children
      softly sparkling here and there.
Like glittering waterfalls
      we flow and spread everywhere.

We are cosmic children
      born to this earth
We are God's children—
      children of the universe.

Music in Silence

Heavenly Mountain, June 2001

Striking the tones of silence
   music gently starts to flow.
Silence is purest harmony—
   all frequencies in synchronous glow.
As Self stirs this tender stillness
   sound subtly begins to hum.
In superfluid gentle swings
   silent strings softly strum.
As Self hears its own song
   consciousness begins to dance
to the music of its own nature—
   the melody of blissful resonance.

Music

Heavenly Mountain, June 2001

Music takes you to a place
  larger than you—
a vast, vibrant space
  magical and true
where tender emotions
  rise and swell
forming musical notions
  from the divine well.
The more delicate your heart
  the purer the sound
the more effective your art—
  deeper and more profound.
Music takes you to silence
  where God sings.
Floating in His alliance
  eternal music springs.

Life's Romance

Heavenly Mountain, May 2001

When I fell in love with my Being
   life's romance began.
Like honey softly streaming
   in life's sweetness I ran.
With open arms everywhere
   I embraced each leaf and flower—
the daffodils that shone fair,
   the honeysuckle's fragrant power.
Now on top of the world in love's elation
   my voice sings its heart's delight
as I spin amongst the field's carnations
   in the freedom of my inner light.
In my own love I am blessed
   for now my love loves everything.
In infinity's vastness I sweetly rest
   at peace, flying on true love's wings.

An Island

Heavenly Mountain, December 2000

I stand on an island
    surrounded by waters
        of clearest turquoise.

I stand on the sand
    with grass cliff borders
        in silent, reflective poise.

The wind is my fan—
    the music, the sea
        the only audible noise.

I am an island
    surrounded by soft air
        of clear transparency.

The universe is so grand.
    Stars surround me
        as I gaze upon galaxies.

Each man is an island
    with his own sea
        that stretches to infinity.

The Chosen Ones

Heavenly Mountain, January 2001

Out of five billion people
               Come
                     you are a chosen one.
Rise like a steeple
               Run
                     into the golden sun.

Alight with transparent wings
               Explore
                     the vast cosmic shore.
With the angels sing
               Pour
                     your heart's tender core.

Chosen to transcend
               Deep
                     to awake from sleep
Chosen to comprehend and
               Reap
                     the bliss of God's keep.

With the celestials gather

      Glide

           on the incoming tide.

On the sea's foamy lather

      Guide

           man to his better side.

Special chosen ones

      Behold

           the royal silent road

Your purity has won

      The gold

           of Heaven's divine abode.

A Silence Poem

Heavenly Mountain, January 2001

Suddenly the earth dropped beneath me.
There I stood—suspended—free
in a vast space of 360 degrees
so pure, so sure
of my own silent eternity.

Suddenly the space melted into streams.
There I stood, no, not in a dream
but in a realm of white vibrant beams—
this glow, I know
is my inner soul redeemed.

Suddenly the rays began to spin
into spirals—some thick, some thin—
curving to their smallest point within.
I unlocked the paradox
of my silence in perpetual motion.

Suddenly I heard a whispering hum—
silence singing in my vast sanctum.
To its song I sweetly succumbed—
clear tones, my own
Self's pulsating continuum.

Suddenly the vastness became still.
There I stood completely fulfilled.
From silence, bliss I distilled.
This space, God's grace,
is the essence of His divine will.

Silence

Holland, January 2000

Silent streams of silence
      weave a silent cadence—
a self-interacting symphony
      where the observer just observes
the flowing silence that curves
      into spirals of perfect symmetry.

Silence spinning its sound
      through spiraling around
spins into impulses of thousands of pieces.
      Silence melts like snow
into rivers that flow
      into silence's sound that increases.

Silence pouring in on itself
      blissfully plays in stealth
like ripples moving across a lake.
      Silence sings its own song
that can be heard, strong
      when silence to itself awakes.

As silence surfaces through the senses
      into perception, silence dances
touching life with its soft veil.
      Silence moves, sweet and serene
yet vibrant on each visual scene—
      this silence I reverently hail.

As Love Stands Still

Holland, January 1999

The river of time goes on and on
unhindered
as love stands still
smiling.

The softness of silence speaks
volumes unheard
as love stands still
smiling.

Seasons circle round and round
winter to fall
as love stands still
smiling.

The birds joyfully sing
nature's songs
as love stands still
smiling.

Merge your breath with stillness
where love resides;
stand still in love
smiling.

Where Does Heaven Begin?

Holland, August 1999

The airbrush-streaked sky
of soft pinks touches the trees.
Where does Heaven end?
Where does Earth begin?
I cannot see.

The crystal clear, cool lake
reflects the shimmering sun.
What is Earth?
What is Heaven?
I question.

The trees blowing in the soft wind
speak the stillness of the eve.
Is this Earth
or is this Heaven?
I cannot perceive.

My own silence mingles with the air
as my joy spills from within me
creating Heaven
on this earth
for my silence is divinity.

What is outside my Self
is mirrored inside of me.
Heaven is on Earth,
and Earth is Heaven
as Heaven is my inner reality.

Lamp at the Door

Holland, April 1999

I am standing at a closed door—
one side darkness, the other side light.
I open the door, the light pours
into the darkness with all its might.

I push the door fully open
and suddenly a thousand rays
shatter the darkness until broken
as light rushes through the archway.

To the outer darkness I gladly call,
"Goodbye to you where I once stayed."
I humbly enter and to my knees fall—
for this moment so many times I prayed.

I look up into the luminous blaze
that sweetly envelops me.
All around is a soft, golden haze—
angelic sparkles are all I see.

I close my eyes and bask in this moment
but the light continues to brightly grow—
fervent as the sun in its ascent
yet soft as the full moon's glow.

I realize that deep in my core
this door never again will close.
I am now a bright lamp at the door
lighting the world from my silent repose.

Standing at the door my light shines
lighting the darkness of diversity.
My rays stretch in long wavy lines
binding darkness to the light of unity.

As a bright lamp at the door
both sides I joyously illuminate
filling all life more and more
with a light that never can dissipate.

Lighting the day with my light,
lighting the night with the day,
I light everything in my sight—
everything near and far away.

I stand at the door's threshold
as a lamp fulfilling its cosmic role—
lighting inner and outer with shimmering gold
igniting Heaven from within my whole.

One Drop of Love
Holland, February 1999

One drop of love—
    angels come down to record it.
Many small drops of love
    ever grow bit by bit
until they become
    one huge swelling ocean
enveloping the world
    with loving, peaceful emotion.

One ounce of love
    to angels weighs a ton—
more valuable than gold
    so all the angels run
to catch it together
    and lift it to the sky.
In celestial formation
    they spread it as they fly.

One drop of peace—
    angels come down to spread it.
Spreading peace
    angels will never quit.
Each tiny particle
    the angels will never miss
for a particle of peace to angels
    is a mountain of bliss.

A ray of peace
    brings the sunshine of hope—
the golden light
    that to the earth slopes,
down which joyfully
    the angels slide
gently catching each peaceful beam
    that within us abides.

One drop of happiness
    is to angels a mighty shower.
All angels delight to catch it
    each second, minute, and hour.
Twenty-four hours
    the angels rejoice as they find
every tiny spark of joy
    on this earth, within mankind.

For all the angels know
    that happiness, love, and peace
are man's very essence
    and in time will increase.
As man looks within
    the angels he will see
as thousands of sparkles
    of his own love, peace, and divinity.

What Really Matters

Holland, January 1999

Does matter really matter
when it is born to dissolve?
Why climb the long ladder?
Why try and evolve?
Matter matters in the matterless,
which we are born to discover.
The ladder's climb becomes effortless
when matter's illusion is uncovered.
Beyond matter, beyond the atom,
beyond the nucleus, beyond time,
beyond space into Self's ashram
discover matter's matterless prime.
This is what truly matters
in one's time here on earth.
Illusion you must shatter
to fulfill the purpose of your birth.
The primal substance of existence,
the primal substance of our soul,
sweetly moves without resistance—
superfluid, unbounded, whole.
Matter is finite, boundaries,
always changing as the tide;
matterless is infinite, floating free
enjoying true freedom's boundless ride.

What really does matter
is that reality is not matter at all
and that life is growing happier, not sadder
in the matterless Home of Natural Law.

Silence

Holland, January 1999

A time of silence
  without speaking a word
yet silence itself
  is loudly heard
as delicate chimes
  ringing crystal clear—
the pure essence
  of matter, space, air.
I hear matter
  collapse like a wave
into a vibrating vastness,
  a reverberating enclave
of light particles
  that dance and spin
whose first stirring
  begins deep within.
These particles bind
  to form matter
creating sound
  like the rain's pitter-patter.
Tonight the moon
  is full and clear.
It is wonderful
  to be still and hear
the tender humming
  louder than a breeze

roaring even fuller
  than the rustling leaves.
A deeper truth
  I hear inside
in the silence
  that rolls like the tide.
All outer noise
  is a fleeting whisper
to the inner quiet
  that rings crisper
as the Almighty
  resounding His hum
calling us to be
  in His silent sanctum.

A Winter Day

Holland, December 1998

The snowy white and silver
    sparkling on the tree's bough
slice a serene, scenic sliver
    in the eternity of now.
The soft white powder
    shimmers in the air
as the wind stirs louder
    the silence spreads everywhere.
The world around me glistens
    as the snowflakes flutter down.
To the hum of silence I listen—
    the pristine purity that abounds.
What can be more pure
    than a fresh sheet of snow
whose silence is its allure
    along with the peace it bestows.
My own warm silence meets
    the cool silence surrounding me,
which melts into a vast sheet
    of thunderous silence—supreme felicity.

Is Man Truly Free?

Holland, December 1998

Is man truly free
    or is life ruled by destiny
alway influenced
    by the confluence
of many forces
    that like a river course
through the cosmos
    in which we are enclosed?
The moon's cyclic spin
    affects tides rolling in
and distant, stately Saturn
    our every turn
along with Mars
    floating in the stars.
We live in a sphere
    with influences everywhere.
The seeds we sow
    are what we bestow
to the atmosphere
    carrying love or fear.
Then we reap
    our own effects that seep
through the air
    touching us with hate or care.
We are entwined
    in influences that wind

throughout our life
    bringing joy or strife.
Actions of hate
    bind one's fate
in an imprisoned cell
    of one's own-made hell.
Life is our own making
    for our own taking.
If goodness we give
    then goodness we live.
Hate never heave
    then love you will receive.
Be always kind—
    your life will shine
in true freedom
    in Heaven's kingdom.
Then you will rise
    above influences of any size,
walking in a sacred land
    held gently by God's hand.

Life's Cosmic Play

Holland, October 1998

Sometimes life feels like a play.
When the last act is over and done
We will look at each other and say,
"Life ended almost as soon as it had begun."
Life is short, and now that it is too late
We will realize that our acts were small
And regrettably sometimes filled with hate—
Acts undeserving of a curtain call.

Life could have been a beautiful show
And still can be filled with laughter and light
By making all men friends, not foes
With each actor like a star in the night.
Let the show now begin anew.
Let the velvet curtain quickly rise.
Let the stage sparkle like drops of dew.
Let the show begin by closing our eyes.

The world stage is not the show to see.
The greatest scene in silence is seen
Where Self acts uninhibited and free
With the royal dignity of a queen.
Inside, actor acts on Self's own stage
Performing its Self-referral cosmic play
Singing the score of silence's page
Commanding a performance of grand display.

Inside one sees entertainment that is pure
With a cast of stars enjoying their roles.
For eternity this show will endure
As it encompasses the universal studio.
Here every part sweetly sings in accord
With the harmonious song of Nature's rule.
Bliss will be one's own reward—
The drama of Self spiraling like a whirlpool.

Dance on the stage of your Being —
The grand theater of open, soft air.
Buy the ticket where you will be seeing
Your Self appear here, there, everywhere.
Enjoy watching Self be directed by itself
To move and swing in all possibilities.
Self has many diverse faces to tell—
The story of its own unified reality.

We are actors on the world stage
But don't get caught in life's illusion.
Play your part like a wise sage.
Go beyond the world's confusion.
Let your life be one happy show
That always has a happy end.
Let your stage be a vibrant rainbow
With angels as your audience of friends.

This cosmic show must always go on
With stars and moon clapping along
Performing from sunset to golden dawn
With a choir singing its celestial song.
Every song will inspire an encore
With everyone in standing ovation.
Flower petals from Heaven will pour
On this stage of God's creation.

Be in the Moment
Holland, October 1998

Man always sits on time's edge—
standing on its thin ledge
where he can slip into a net of the past
or fall into dreams of a future that casts
dream after dream after dream
for his life to be redeemed.
Or he can stand in the present's threshold—
in the gap beyond the hold
of a past that is no more
or of a future's unreal, unopened door.

In the gap between future and past
discover eternity's song that lasts
as the sweetness of one's own silence—
Being—in the present's alliance.
Living in the present shapes days of yore
into sweet memories to adore.
Being here now, the future shines
making dreams reality each moment in time.

Living in the past only covers
the beauty of now that always hovers.
Living in the future also hides
the beauty of now that in silence resides.
Right now is the most precious time.

Right here and now, life tenderly chimes
with the soft echo of eternity
that rings in the gap between past and future—
immortality.

Look in the Mirror

Holland, August 1998

Look in the mirror, what do you see?
If you see pure tranquility
you are seeing your self centered—
your own Self who can enter
its own reflection.

Look in the mirror, what do you see?
If you see a stormy sea
you are not seeing your Self clear;
you are not seeing one who is dear—
only surface contradictions.

Look in the mirror without dust.
See your Self shine free and just.
All life is your reflection.
All life is your own projection
waiting to mirror Self's perfection.

As the Wind Blows

Holland, April 1998

As the wind blows swiftly,
  invisible, soft, and warm,
my spirit to Heaven lifts
  riding the breeze of transparent form.
Through the galaxies my soul drifts
  where stars sparkle in clustering swarms;
my Being embraces the supreme gift
  free from clouds and fearful storms.
As a flickering light constantly shifts
  Self sees itself perform.
In Self's depths I am never adrift—
  to God's law I joyously conform.

Poetry of Silence
Holland, May 1998

A poet captures moments in time—
truths, eternity, to put in rhyme—
going beyond matter into feeling
into his inner depths revealing
the poetry of silence.

A painter paints life in vivid color;
poets paint words in metaphor.
Painters break form into light particles;
poets make words sing like canticles—
the poetry of silence.

Composers hear music in every sound
creating song when rhythm is found.
Poets hear life as spoken words
weaving their meter into measures heard—
the poetry of silence.

Pure white canvas is colored with paint
in colors lucid or colors faint
as the artist reveals his inward seeing.
Forms in his heart he is freeing—
the poetry of silence.

Pure white sheet is covered in similes
in symbolism, imagery, and in reveries.
A poet bares his innermost thoughts
that rise from his depths and have caught
the poetry of silence.

My Home

Holland, May 1998

I live in a home
without any walls,
without ceiling domes
or long, winding halls;
without any floors
or any rooms,
not even doors
for me to walk through.

My home
is cozy and warm.
I live and roam
safe from storms.
I am enclosed
by walls of space.
My windows
open to every place.

Heaven is my mansion,
my ceiling, the sky
of infinite dimension
where no one can pry.
My house is lit by stars,
illumined by the sun.
My house is not far
but within everyone.

Come home and rest
on a bed of air—
a golden net
spread everywhere.
Enjoy pure luxury
in this kingdom
beyond all worry
when home you come.

Take Only One Road

Holland, May 1998

There are many roads to take,
many directions to go,
many skies to fly,
many oceans to row.

There are many hills to climb,
many paths to follow,
many rivers to cross,
but their ends are shallow.

Take only one path—
one joyous road.
Let all travel converge
in Self's heavenly abode.

Let go of outer direction.
Let Self be your guiding hand.
The purpose of any journey
is to end in God's land.

You will end up there
after many mountains crossed.
Cut short your long journey
on useless paths getting lost.

The way is simple, effortless,
faster than a jet plane.
Let your compass point you within
to Heaven's domain.

Never swerve from your path—
always stay on course.
You will arrive in a flash
in Heaven—your own silent source.

Go Beyond

Holland, May 1998

I have to break away
        from my usual rhyming schemes
and portray
words that sway
        a more meaningful theme.

I have to let go
        of phrases always used
and show
pure as snow
        a truer expression of my muse.

I have to go beyond
        my usual train of thought
and wave a wand
to create a bond
        for you magically to get caught.

I have to be more innovative
        finding new words to rhyme
more celebrative
and creative
        creating profundities each time.

I have to dive deep
            and probe my heart and mind
to awake from sleep
and from silence reap
            the words to bless mankind.

To God I have to humbly kneel
            and touch love's fine emotions
and deeply feel
what He reveals
            and put His words in motion.

Speak the Sweet Truth

Holland, May 1998

If you speak ill of others
you speak ill of yourself.
Your own ills you uncover—
the mud hiding in stealth.

If your heart is open and pure
no ill words could ever slip.
Words will be a soothing cure
and nectar will fall from your lips.

If you can't say something nice
then better not say anything at all.
Even thinking ill is a bad vice—
bad thoughts pierce the thickest of walls.

Words hold great power—
their intonations even more.
Let them be sweet, not sour
opening the heart, not closing its door.

Kind words always uplift
elevating the atmosphere.
Let your words always be a gift
spreading kindness everywhere.

Your heart will find its purity
when beyond all thought you go.
Silence speaks with greatest maturity—
only kindness can silence bestow.

Let your silence speak free
singing its inward pleasure.
Your silence holds the gentle key
to words of endless treasure.

Muse, You Have Come Again

Holland, May 1998

O muse, my dear friend
you have graciously come again.
Let the new day happily begin
with your words flowing through my pen.

What you will say this morn
I need not even ponder.
I love to watch your words be born
when to my Self I wander.

Your words come right on cue,
as to an actor in a play
bringing truth in rainbow hues
when in silence I stay.

Like bubbles rising from a well
your words flow through my hand
that writes everything you tell
in color vivid, never bland.

When I forget you for a second
and put down my writing pen
then to me you always beckon
to come out and play again.

Dear muse, today your words unfurl
like a gushing fountain or swirling pool.
May each word be a sapphire, ruby, or pearl
containing wisdom in every jewel.

Muse, I adore it when you come.
I want to capture every phrase.
In silence you and I become
one hand to write God's praise.

Dear Muse

Holland, May 1998

Please let me rest, dear muse
the night is no longer young;
yet I cannot refuse
the words pouring from your tongue.

They whisper such sweetness
I can hardly bear their joy.
Your words are always kindness
and playful like a toy.

But the night is getting late.
Do you want to take my sleep?
Let your flow quickly abate;
now I should be counting sheep.

The time is after ten
but you are tireless, wanting to play.
Please let me lay down my pen.
Don't keep me up till break of day.

Dear muse, adorable friend
I love it when you come.
Your entertainment's without end.
I delight in your whispering hums.

But to bring you full glory
I must get my night's rest
then your words will be purer allegory
and I will be feeling my best!

Poetry in Motion
Holland, April 1998

See pure poetry in motion—
form expressing deep emotion
as rhythms rippling 'cross the ocean
rising in waves of devotion.

See pure love swirl
and spiral into its own curl
entwined in the eternal twirl
soft and gentle as a pearl.

See pure oneness flow—
free as the air that blows
smooth as ice in sparkling glow
graceful like a gentle doe.

See pure love dance
elegant in its prance
dynamic and silent in stance
leaving no step to chance.

Life is love in motion—
its swing is poetry's notion
its oneness beyond commotion
its dance throws silence into motion.

Skate upon love's lake
where life is glittering, awake
where the flow is without break
where love is lived for God's sake.

Golden Flute

Holland, January 1998

Hear the golden flute's trills
as they spill
and thrill
all creation
with their reverberation
reaching the ends of the universe
bringing Heaven back to earth.

Hear the golden flute resound
with notes spinning round
which abound
as cosmic dance
in gentle resonance
touching each scintillating star
as it travels near and far.

Hear the golden flute's descant
as it chants
and enchants
with its refrain
in notes sustained
throughout the firmament
with soft allurement.

Hear the golden flute sing
as it rings
and brings
harmonious variation
in subtle intonation—
the symphony of the cosmos
with its many soft cantos.

Hear the golden flute's call
out to all
to gently fall
into its hum
so we become
one with its psalm—
soothing, gentle, and calm.

Hear the song of the flute
as it constitutes
the Absolute
vibrating within itself
eternally sounding in stealth
like the echoes in a silent cave—
our stillness moving in sound waves.

Hear the golden flute's tone
in soft drones
of our own
tender peace
from matter released
where only frequencies exist—
our own Self-referral bliss.

I Write for My Self

Holland, August 1997

I write for my own elation
to feel tender bubbles arise in me
and burst into poetic creation
rising from my silent sea.

I hear a voice that does not sound
murmuring its meaning in abstraction.
Silence hears silence's gentle pound
from Self turning in inward contraction.

I hear a music that is not heard
which plays my heart strings
forming melody into rhythmic word,
touching my feelings as it sings.

I write for my Self,
for Self sings its own song inside
where sound and form wait in stealth
for me to unleash their rhythmic tide.

As voice and sound become one stream
my heart opens to its rushing flow,
which contains in its rhyming schemes
Self seeing its own glittering glow.

Graduation

Holland, December 1997

Every day is a graduation
to new ideas, new heights
to soar free in imagination
discovering one's Self in that flight.

Let us graduate anew each day
and sail upon life's changing seas;
be not tossed by storms on the way—
beyond the clouds fly free.

Let us graduate, everyone;
but what are we graduating to?
We are graduating to become
our own Self—that which is true.

Life is just our own vision—
our own dreams to fulfill.
March forward with focused precision
and climb the highest hill.

Live each day with joyous hearts;
capture life's precious goal.
We must graduate beyond the parts
into the cosmic whole.

Then our diploma is well deserved—
when we are an inspiration
ready to uplift and serve
our families, country, and all nations.

May our graduation never end;
every day, may we continue to grow.
Let the whole world be our friend;
let us bless life with our own golden glow.

Sunset

Holland, July 1997

Pink, pastel-soft evening streaks
airbrush the baby-blue sky.
The misty crescent moon's dawning peak
soothes me as I sleepily lie
in awe of this magical moment
that sends me off to sleep.
In this moment is Heaven's descent
that captures me in God's keep.
Drawn into the beauty of God's display
I awake to His perfect universe.
I am caught in His eternal play—
the silence that structures Heaven on Earth.

I Am the Universe

Holland, June 1997

In the seed I am the tree
In the sap I am the flower
In the drop I am the sea
In the second I am the eternal hour

In the grain I am the sand
In the speck I am the earth
In the particle I am the land
In the atom I am the universe

In the matter I am space
In the boundaries I am free
In the thread I am the lace
In my Self I am Totality

In the micro I am the macro
In the sprinkle I am the rain
In the stop I am the flow
In my Self I am in God's domain

Sing Songbirds

Holland, May 1997

Fill this sanctuary with your trills.
Thrill me with your songs until
I sing with you
and soar into
Heaven.

Enchant me with your descant.
Chant gently until I can't
bear the bliss
in the soft mist
of Heaven.

Sing your songs of spring.
Ring clear and bring
songs that resound
with the bliss that abounds
in Heaven.

Call all men and enthrall.
Stall them into silent fall.
Close their eyes
let them realize
Heaven.

Troubadours of bliss, you we adore.
Your songs fly into our core
of soft serenity
stirring the felicity
of Heaven.

From Oneness

Holland, May 1997

From one sea of silence, all music flows.
From one vast ocean, all waves dance.
From one green field, all plants grow.
Upon one expanse, stars shine in radiance.
From one air, all winds blow.
Upon one cosmic strand, man takes his stance.

In one blue sky, birds spread their wings.
From one clay, a potter molds his form.
From one soft sand, all castles spring.
From one seed, a tree is born.
From one unity, diversity sings.
From one intelligence, life is ever transformed.

Let us swing in the song of silence.
Let us sink in the ocean's calm.
Let us know the field's science.
Let us hear the wind's psalm.
Let us in the expanse gain reliance.
Let us live on Natural Law's alms.
Let us with the Eternal One be in alliance.

In Silence I Hear

Holland, March 1997

Tell me your wise words
Dictate them sweetly to me.
Let them come like a rushing herd
Or waves rolling on the sea.

My mind is still and clear
Like the depths of a crystal pond.
In this silence I gently hear
Your words softly coming on.

In metaphors, in rhythmic rhyme
They flow like a stream.
Rising in my awareness they climb
Forming the poetry of the Supreme.

God is silence, the Absolute—
The beauty of Heaven's kingdom.
Here His words flow like notes from a flute.
In my peace, I hear His wisdom.

Morning Birds

Holland, April 1997

With your whistles awake the world
as you one by one join in the chorus.
Let the morning joys unfurl
as you sing your songs for us.

Reverberating through the misty air
sound your sweet and gentle trills.
Your songs are a morning prayer
awakening our hearts to God's will.

Sing, morning birds
along with the cuckoo's steady beat;
let the dove's coos be heard
soothing man into Self-retreat.

Let the alluring voice of the larks
resonate up to the endless sky
making the world an enchanted park
with their singing, hovering high.

Even the cawing of the crow
blends in with perfect harmony
like violins and chimes in rhythmic crescendo
weaving a jubilant symphony.

Fill our days with your descants,
your arias and hymns of the Divine
so all darkness now recants
and Heaven reveals its melodious sign.

Heaven on Earth is your song—
wake all men to ummistakably hear.
Help them to see the golden dawn
with each note that rings pure and clear.

Fill the trees, fill the universe
with your songs as you soar.
Awaken all men to cosmic verse
so once again God all men adore.

Cherry Tree

Holland, April 1997

Spring, bring your sweet cherry blossoms
bursting into soft clouds of white
renewing our minds each time they come
to the magic of Being with their magical sight.

Each precious tree's unfolding flowers
fulfill spring's sacred duty
to invoke love's delicate power—
love of life's inner and outer beauty.

What is that magic that within you lies
giving us such soft sensuality?
You are the purest feast for our eyes
as we savor your divine reality.

As we walk beneath your silken petals
that gently fall to the ground below
our hearts and minds smoothly settle
to that sweetness you bestow.

Your sap is of virtuous essence;
its intelligence is awake to God's hand.
Your loveliness cannot be by chance
for you are a strong player in God's plan.

You are placed in His cosmic design
to inspire devotion to His creation
to bring our hearts to be Self-aligned
with Self's seasonless, perpetual celebration.

Cherry tree covered in delicate lace
you are spring's song kindling hope
that all men of every creed and race
will awake to life's cosmic scope

and blossom in their own inner sanctum
like your blossoms of noble gentility
and be the person they were meant to become—
a reflection of God's divinity.

Heaven's Kingdom

Holland, April 1997

Seek first Heaven's Kingdom
and all else will be given to you.
Gain the pinnacle of life's sum
in this soft, misty place of golden hue.

In simplicity Thy Kingdom comes
like a fresh breeze of early spring.
In this paradise sweetly hums
the only song worthy to sing.

Silence is the song of this land
for silence sings the reign of right.
Love is silence's royal command—
in love one surrenders to greater heights.

Heaven is life's innermost core—
the still place within one's heart.
Go inside, knock, open the door;
from this center let your life start.

No longer live from life's hard edge;
life's only life if lived from its center.
In silence make your sacred pledge
then Heaven's door you will enter.

As Heaven's door opens feel the thrill;
let your eyes swell with joyful tears.
In silence you have awakened God's will
beyond duality, beyond all fear.

In Heaven's palace you are served
every desire, every glory divine.
Within your stillness never swerve—
with God you will be ever aligned.

Mr. President
Holland, April 1997

Here you stand
    in the long corridor of time
where woman and man
    have rung the bells that chime
        history in the making.
With your hand
    our nation will climb
to the shoreless sands
    where nothing can bind
        self-government awaking.
Under Natural Law's command
    you will redefine
the glory of our land
    to be pristine and shine
        vast and breathtaking.

You know true power
    is making enemies friends.
If war should shower
    life will inexcusably end
        and no one wins.
You know true power
    is in peaceful amends
where life will flower
    and life will defend
        life without sin.

Life will tower
    and peace will ascend
to the golden hour
    and joy will descend
        to man within.

You will lead
    by Natural Law's light
a silent creed
    with might of right
        putting wrong in rejection
fulfilling the need
    of each man's plight
to joyfully succeed
    and regain his sight
        of pious direction.
Nothing can impede
    your noble fight
for ignorance to recede
    and man to alight
        in heavenly perfection.

Grandfather

Holland, March 1997

Grandfather, grand like a mountain
you stood tall in our eyes—
joyful, bubbling like a fountain
always royal, humble, and wise.

Like the vast rolling ocean
was your noble life's vision.
Your family you held in devotion
guiding with loving supervision.

As the gentle monarch of our clan
you reigned firm and supreme
rising above the common man
fulfilling life's highest dream.

You taught us that life's joys
exist in the simple things—
family, friends, girls and boys,
evening walks, hearing birds sing.

You taught us never to forget
our spirituality, our Lord.
For only in God can we net
life's most fulfilling and deepest reward.

You stood for that which is true.
You gave in humble anonymity.
Our generation is blessed by you,
and your gracious generosity.

Thinking of you our lives lift
to greater heights of fortitude.
Knowing your goodness is our truest gift
for your life was one of beatitude.

Reflecting on Dad

Holland, March 1997

How blessed and fortunate we were
to have your joy fill our hearts
and the wisdom that you conferred
to us to stand strong and start
on our own life's journey.

As our journey proceeds each mile
your warmth inside us is still alive.
Thinking of you brings a smile
giving us strength as we strive
to fulfill our own destiny.

The memory of you is steadfast
as you are what we came from.
You are the light of our past
and of our future as we grow to become
the fullness you represent.

From father to child, child to father
quickly spins life's eternal wheel.
As we circle round may we uncover
life's inner beauty that you revealed
in your own contentment.

As a wheel's spokes are bound to its core
with you we keep our bond.
As we go through life's many doors
in our hearts you will always live on
in tender affection.

In our deep silence we will see
our timeless connection in eternity.
Sailing through life's changing seas
we joyfully seek our own divinity
holding you in reflection.

Never Stop Singing

Holland, January 1997

Life could not exist without song—
the setting sun, the golden dawn,
the swelling ocean and rivers that flow,
the waxing moon casting her soft glow;

flowers blooming, trees swaying,
church bells ringing, a man praying,
each soft breath, every beat of the heart,
the changing display of Nature's art.

Song is life, life is song,
singing as the wind, carrying us along
through rhythms in which we are entwined
in ethereal music of the Divine.

Song is life's delicate essence—
our own silence in effervescence,
the eternal symphony of creation
harmonizing every man and nation.

When we sing, we become one
united in God's Kingdom.
Transcending difference, transcending race
in song we transcend time and space.

It is Nature's language all can sing—
fall, winter, summer and spring,
the crystal clarity of a cool lake,
our Being, our Self, fully awake.

Never stop singing or the day will end.
Sing your heart, sing dear friend.
I will sing too, full and clear
but first we must be still and hear.

In our own silence deeply immersed
flows the music of the universe,
in our hearts, in tender emotion,
rushing in rivers, and the rolling ocean.

Hear it pulsating in twinkling stars,
throbbing in the sun shimmering afar.
Hear it humming as our Self within,
the angelic song of the Kingdom of Heaven.

Sing your silence every precious day
in praise of the morn's first sparkling ray.
Sing, sing, and Heaven you will bring.
Never stop singing, sing, sing, sing.

Hear the Music of Poetry
Holland, December 1996

Think deeply and hear creation's song
in meter and the silence between each beat—
a soft timbre of tones, full and strong
in which all sound frequencies are replete.

Let the poet recall the depths of his mind
in words, emotions, in rhythms that dance
into imagery, metaphor, and phrases that wind
his silence into meanings condensed.

Summon your experiences fresh from Being;
evoke life's passions from your heart.
Let your words carry the sound of meaning
then the poet will have achieved his art.

Capture the music of the universe
your ear tuned to the voice of sound.
In your silence deeply immersed
your expressions will be eternally profound.

If you think deeply, you think musically
hearing stillness in tones crystal-clear—
the poetry of Self's own rhapsody—
God's song most pleasing to hear.

Create Beauty Every Moment
Holland, December 1996

The wise never dwell on the past
neither good nor bad times.
They know outer situations never last
like a river that endlessly winds
past banks of unending change.

More powerful than past is present.
Be fully awake here and now.
Create beauty out of every moment.
In the present let your life bow
to the joy of life's full range.

Don't succumb to your life as fate.
Create your destiny every step of the way.
Step only through a righteous gate;
sweetly move in pious sway
thus gaining glories divine.

You create your past and future
by how you live your present.
Live your eternal, Self-referral nature
beyond life's changing events—
beyond delusion—in Heaven's shrine.

The Winds of Heaven

Holland, August 1996

Hear the song of the wind
rustling through the leaves
thrilling my silence within
as it flows through me.

Your whisper sings in softest tones
rolling like a swelling ocean
humming in soothing drones
touching my deepest emotions.

Your winds play like a flute
whose notes echo in the air
or like the strings of a lute
which reverberate everywhere.

All forms melt into your sound
swinging with your rising pitch.
I become lost but then found
in your tones deep and rich.

Losing myself in your song
my heart becomes sweetly filled
with a murmur that carries me along
in harmony with God's will.

The more I give in and surrender
to your gentle, harmonious measures,
the more you overtake me and render
God's melodious treasures.

God sings softly in the wind—
listen to His quiet words
which hum as Self within—
here the winds of Heaven are heard.

Year in Being
Holland, May 1996

Spill the stillness of January—
delicate snowflakes like sparkling fairies
blanket life in shimmering peace.
Be blessed in the coolness of February—
settling, silent, and solitary—
in which life's hustle has ceased.

Swing on the wings of March
carrying one above its melting arch
that curves into spring's awakening.
Let the showers flower into April's
tulips, hyacinths, and daffodils
spreading the sweetness each blossom brings.

Hear the whispers conferred in May—
the morning birds heralding the day
in a grand chorus of jubilance.
Feel the breeze of the eves of June—
soft and balmy atop the sand dunes—
that hums in gentle cadence.

Unwind your mind in timeless July.
Soar free like birds that smoothly fly
beneath the warm, vibrant sunshine.
Hold God's hand on the the sands of August.
Be led into His waters—kind and just—
in the sapphire ocean of the Divine.

Return to the taciturn September.
Come home to Being and remember
Self's seasonal transformations.
Fall into the call of October
whose golden leaves are soon over
in winter's coming hibernation.

Be replete in the retreat of November
into your scintillating silence that renders
sacredness beyond all reason.
Transcend into the friend of December—
pure as snow, yet warm and tender—
completing the yearly cycle of day, month, and season.

Blessed Unity

Holland, May 1996

What union can be more blessed
than the union with one's silence?
Fulfill love's supreme quest
by gaining this universal alliance.
In love dwells God's power.
His strength lies in tenderness.
Abiding in Him, His love showers
delicate drops of gentleness.
As rivers melt into one ocean
merging together in one silent sea
surrender in waves of deep emotion
that rise and lift one to be free.
In unity love is truly free
becoming frictionless in its purity.
In silence is love's sacred key
that unlocks the door to highest felicity.
May your every step be in unison
moving in time with the cosmic dance.
Fly on love's wings into the sun
floating as one in Self's expanse.
In one's vast Self only true love sings
its warm, soft song of eternity.
Awake in Being love sweetly sings
the holy purpose of blessed unity.

The World is as We Are

Holland, April 1996

Our mind is the creator of our world
thus creator and creation are one.
The world is our own thoughts unfurled
creating rough waves or the calm ocean.

If we wear grey glasses we see grey—
the world is as we are.
Wear golden glasses and see a golden day—
the world shining as a brilliant star.

Our mind is like a window—dusty or clear.
Clear, it creates a world of gold.
Clear, it reflects Self's golden sphere—
a sparkling world for you to behold.

Clear the dusty window of your mind
by transcending to Self's transparent sea.
Then no dust can hide or bind
your Being shining its full glory.

Clearing our mind of confusion
Self sweetly reflects its purity—
dispelling mirage, dispelling illusion—
and creates a world of God's divinity.

Swing

Holland, February 1996

Swing in the cradle of creativity
    between point and infinity.
Swing in the cradle of God
    and with your churning rod
        stir the ocean of wholeness.

Swing between dynamism and silence;
    be cradled in God's alliance.
Swing on the lap of mother
    comforted by her light that uncovers
        your sparkling wakefulness.

In tender stillness sweetly oscillate
    in the bliss that scintillates
illuminating the universe
    where pulsating points converse—
        the humming of Totality.

Sway in delicate reverberations.
    Hear Nature's gentle intonations
as Self's measured tone
    where knower knows the known:
        the song of immortality.

Swing on the seat spread everywhere.
    Rise on the cushion of soft air.
Float into your ecstasy
    in Self-referral rhapsody
        sparkling like a snowflake.

In and out joyfully swing.
As flying angels, stretch your wings
embracing all God's creation
    in tender Self-revelation—
        your Being fully awake.

Palm Trees

Holland, January 1996

Palm trees, palm trees
swaying in the breeze
whispering in the wind
whispering with the sea
rolling out and in.

Palm trees, palm trees
your long, folded leaves
rustling in the air
make man free
from the hustle everywhere.

Palm trees, palm trees
sing all you please.
What is your tune
you serenade to me
and to the full moon?

Palm trees, palm trees
swinging with ease
your song is a psalm
soothing all to be
joyful and calm.

Beyond Change
Holland, April 1996

Life always moves in change
from spring to fall's colorful range.
Friends and loved ones come and go
with the wind that unseen blows.

On outer situations never depend
for momentary joys come to an end.
Your happiness must come from inside
beyond change's changing tides.

Be anchored to your silent core
like a boat anchored to the ocean floor.
Be not tossed by life's changing seas.
In your calm let your life sail free.

Men may come and men may go
but one's inner silence eternally flows.
Skate on this river smooth as ice
beyond change into Self's paradise.

Awake
Holland, January 1996

Arise from your sleep!
Awake to the dawn!
Come into my keep.
Gently leap like a fawn
beyond your intellect
into the dazzling sun
where Self reflects
the infinity it has spun.

Awake to the rays
that stream into your heart
in Self-referral display
in scintillating art
beaming out to the sky
and back within
like a bird darting high
then diving low with the wind.

Dive into the lake
of joyous effervescence
where Self is awake
to its lively expanse.
May all men awake
to their pulsating silence
that sparkles like a snowflake
gaining God's alliance.

Awake, awake and rise.
Open the window within you.
Enjoy with your inner eyes
the bliss dancing in view.
Arise from sleep
from illusion's plight;
Heaven you will reap
fully awake in God's Light.

Can I Capture You?

Holland, 1996

Can I capture you in words?
I would have to make silence heard.
Can I sing your full grace?
My voice would have to reach all space.

Can I capture you in art?
I would have to paint your whole in each part.
Can I capture you in prose?
I would have to describe the entire cosmos.

Can I capture your bubbling bliss?
I would have to know the ocean's fullness.
Can I capture your shimmering light?
I would have to be the stars in the night.

Can I capture you in verse?
I would have to rhyme the universe.
Can I capture your wisdom?
I would have to know Heaven's Kingdom.

Lily

Holland, June 1995

Lily, you lull me to sleep
      with your divine scent.
Lily, I linger in your keep
      curled in my silent crescent.

Lily, lovely like a white star
      glittering at twilight;
Lily, lilting in fields afar—
      the meadows in gold you ignite.

Lily, you light up my day
      with your delicacy.
Lily, listen to what I say—
      you are subtle ecstasy.

Lily, you give your fragrance
      that wafts in the night air.
Lily, loving is your essence
      settling me in your care.

Fulfill Life's Purpose

Holland, November 1995

Sons and daughters, do justice to the life
      your parents lovingly gave you.
Go for the highest, beyond strife
      and seek only that which is true.

The purpose of your birth
      is to discover the Lord.
In your stillness, find his mirth.
      Be bound to his tender cord.

You are a moving universe in stride
      mirroring its structure in each cell.
Stand tall and walk with pride
      harboring all creation within your citadel.

As a seed contains the entire tree
      in the warm fibers of its empty shell,
in silence, you are pulsating frequencies,
      a network of intelligence in swell.

As the intelligence of a flower
      is contained in its sap
the intelligence of your consciousness empowers
      the universal, constitutional map.

Your physiology is a sacred land
       consecrated by your silence—
a woven tapestry of intelligent strands
       moving in universal compliance.

Your body is the temple of the Holy Spirit
       therefore glorify in your body the Lord.
Gain in your life this highest merit—
       the bliss He abundantly affords.

In your calm, His bliss flows freely
       like sap filtering through a plant
carrying the impulse of immortality
       in the humming of silence's chant.

May the purpose of life be fulfilled
       as you fathom your own constitution
as the Constitution of the Universe—God's Will
       bringing supreme Heaven to fruition.

Love and God
Holland, October 1995

Have God's love and enjoy.
    Dance free tied to His thread
that binds in freedom's joy.
    In freedom, love flows as nectar fed
into your heart from His infinite well.

Love is life's greatest mystery
    easily solved in its sacredness.
Sacred is Self's silent sea
    that rises in waves of Self-caress
enveloping one's Being in its swell.

Self in its purity is an ocean—
    a vast reservoir of gentle tides—
one's own wholeness in motion
    where deepest love sweetly abides
and ascends into one's soul.

Self is the supreme Lord—
    the silent Self of everyone.
Love is His eternal reward
    that shines like a thousand suns
making one sovereign and whole.

God's love flows ever free
    if one is open to receive His grace.
Love is God's holy decree
    that each person is free to embrace
in Self-revelation.

Self-Referral Friendship
Holland, October 1995

One's Self one should never degrade
for silent Self is the Lord.
In His waters one should wade
securing His friendship, His reward.

Self should uplift the Self alone.
One should never be forlorn.
Self-doubt should never be sown.
Self-enmity should never be born.

Self is one's own best friend
if one is connected to silence within.
Self is one's enemy when
seated in turbulence, one's tossed by wind.

Subdue your foe, your hostility
by gaining accord with gentle silence.
Win your honor, your nobility
by enjoying your own Self-reliance.

Conquer yourself by your Self.
Triumph in capturing your simplicity.
Procuring peace, victoriously dwell
shielded by Self's invincible purity.

Silent Self can never be a foe
lying beyond conflicting hardship.
Self is love, gentle as a doe
tender in Self-referral friendship.

Self-referral, intimate friend,
may we soar like birds beyond the sun
into Thy light—infinity's end—
basking in the bliss of eternal union.

Play Your Instrument

Holland, May 1995

Play your heart, play your flute,
play your soul, play the absolute;
play your harp, play your strings,
play as delicate as angel wings;
play the dawn, play the night's peace,
play until all sound has ceased.

Play silence with your guitar strum,
play stillness with your gentle drum;
play your calm with a soft violin—
serenity's psalm singing within;
play the dance of joy—the morning sun,
play the bliss sparkling in everyone.

Play your bells, play your tunes,
play the song of stars and the full moon;
play the silence of winter, the awakening of spring,
play along with the birds that sing;
play the rains of April, the evenings of June,
play the water falling into lagoons.

Play your crescendo, play your strain,
play your Self-referral silent domain;
play the rivers, play the vast sea,

play the waves that rise in synchrony;
play the blessed rhythms of eternity,
play Heaven's song within you and me.

Beyond Maya

Holland, March 1995

Maya, casting your spell, casting your charm
You bind all men in your invisible arms.
You perform your play, creating illusions;
For centuries man has been held in your confusion.
You are a dream, a tempting mirage;
Your alluring power works in camouflage.
You are that which does not exist—
But your enchantment is hard to resist.

Maya, how can one let go of you
And go beyond all that is untrue?
How can one awake from your dream
From your powers and be redeemed?
Going beyond all relativity
One is unleashed from your binding activity.
Seated in silence's protective armor
Your power is lost as a charmer.

In silence, Self is securely sealed
Untouched by the spell that you wield.
In Being one freely dances and sings
No longer tightly held by your strings.
Going beyond that which is not
One escapes from your binding knot.
From illusion one is released
And is charmed into purest peace.

Simply by Being, be sweetly enticed
Into your inner wakeful paradise—
A charm greater than the greatest power;
A charm more sweet than a delicate flower.
Into your cosmic Self easily slip;
Be gracefully caught in God's gentle grip.
Align with God's Will, be in Heaven's hold;
Walk free in God's light of shimmering gold.

Fly Free

Holland, March 1995

O bird, sitting in your cage
Fly free like the silence of a sage
Let your wings spread naturally
Be the bird you are meant to be

       Fly free

  O friend, acting on illusion's stage
  Be free like a poet filling his page
  Let your Being spread like a bird's wing
  To all boundaries no longer cling

       Fly free

O bird, soar to endless heights
Let no barriers hinder your flights
Dart above the clouds into the wind
Dive and rise again in playful spin

       Fly free

  O friend, fly into your inner light
  Awake from the darkness of the night
  Greet your new celestial realm
  Sail freely in control of your helm

       Fly free

O bird, sweep through the soft air
With grace, float in sun's fanfare
Never again be unhappily bound
Sing songbird, lift off the ground
                              Fly free

        Friend, listen with deepest care
        Of your silent self be ever aware
        Fly in your stillness beyond all words
        Float free and happy like the songbird
                              Fly free

Silence Call Me
Holland, February 1995

Silence, call me to your abode.
I walk down the joyous road
and climb the highest hill
for the tender thrill
of your solitude.

Silence, call me to your sanctuary
open, free, and solitary.
Let me fly to the sky
light like a butterfly
and float in beatitude.

Silence, call me to your shrine
into the light of the Divine.
Seated upon your altar
I will never falter
safe in your cocoon.

Silence, call me to your universe—
through the galaxies I traverse
swinging from star to star
to know who you are—
sun, sky, and full moon.

Silence, call me to your home
to dwell beneath your sacred dome.
Your walls are my strong brace.
In your rooms I sit encased
within the doors of peace.

Silence, call me to your paradise.
My self to itself I sacrifice
for Heaven to reveal its glory—
Self's own story—
where all darkness has ceased.

Silence, call me to your serenity.
Let me move in your felicity
where angels sing
and crystal bells ring
resounding through your sanctity.

Silence, call me to your sea.
Let me hear your divine decree
and be ordained in your waters
flowing to all quarters
and bathe in your sublimity.

Silence, call me to your silence
where I am in alliance
with the impulse of God's will
moving tranquil
through life's play.

Silence, call me in your light cone
where I spiral to your throne—
a vast network of intelligence
sparkling in effulgence
in royal display.

Silence, call me to your palace
where kindness exists—no malice—
a castle of jeweled splendor
where each gilded room renders
Heaven's reward.

Silence, call me to your cradle;
feed me with your golden ladle.
Fill me from your divine kettle
with nectar that makes me settle
securely in the Lord.

Ode to a Rose

Holland, February 1995

The sweet scent of spring is in the air
As flowers blossom everywhere—
The acacia, hyacinth, and queen among those
The alluring beauty of the regal rose.

Filling the eve with her exotic fragrance
She calms my Being into a peaceful trance.
Casting a spell with her charming power
She reigns supreme among all flowers.

She unfolds her petals of soft symmetry
Like velvet, or a silk-laced tapestry
That climbs and trims each walkway and arch
Enhanced by the delight of the melodic larks.

As peace is symbolized by the dove
She is the symbol of truest love
To be offered in tender devotion
To be sung by the poet's deepest emotion.

But what of the mystery of her thorn?
Doesn't she know only to enchant or adorn?
Does not life consist of opposite extremes?
Does not our attention guide our dreams?

Beauty lies in the beholder's eye—
Enjoy the sun or dwell on the dark sky.
This is the lesson the rose beseeches—
Turn within to your innermost reaches.

For beauty of Self is beauty of the rose
Where no thorn can exist, nor any foes
Only the sap that flows without resistance—
Pure love sweetly nourishing all existence.

I am a rose, you are a rose—
The story of life, the sweetest prose
Whose petals unfold from within
Revealing one's own inner sanctum.

Rose, touching my heart with your beauty
You touch all beings, for your sacred duty
Is to waft the air with your heavenly scent—
You are God's gift with divine intent.

As one walks in your garden of aromatic grace
You sweetly remind the human race
Of the beauty and glory of God's creation—
That life should be lived in celebration.

In reds, peaches, pinks, and golden yellows
You sanctify the ground with hues rich and mellow
Your petals fall as a heavenly rainbow
To carpet the spring in colorful glow.

Royal rose with your perfumed train
All the gods gather to sing your refrain.
Within your seed lies the whole universe—
You are Heaven adorning the earth.

I Am in Love
Holland, May 1994

I am in love
       with the u-ni-verse
with my Being—
       my silence that bursts
into songs freeing
       rhythms embedded in my soul.

I am in love
       as my Self tours
the ocean's calm
       as each wave soars
and settles in psalms
       that swaying silence extols.

I am in love
       with the wind's lullaby
that in the eve hums
       with the power to sanctify
as I succumb
       to its rustling gentle rolls.

I am in love
       with my spirit that runs free
as a river rushes
       along banks of eternity.
Reaching the sea, it hushes
       swinging from depth to shoal.

I am in love
        with the cosmic dance
the waltzing spin—
        Self's radiance
illumined within
        in melodic flickering glow.

I am in love
        secure in the lap
of Divine Mother
        whose love pours as sap
to me and all others
        as hymns of the supreme goal.

I am in love
        with the holy hour
the dawn's descant
        the golden-rayed shower
the awakening bird's chant
        revealing God as my own whole.

Celebrating the Birth of the Lord
A Christmas Poem
Holland, December 1993

Celebrating the birth
of the Lord
whose light on earth
we adore
as Heaven within.

In sweet mirth
we seek His reward
and find His worth
when we move in accord
with His Heaven within.

He is our king
whose salvation
eternally brings
purest elation
in His Heaven within.

As angels' wings
spread in jubilation
in chorus they sing
triumphant laudation
of Heaven within.

Caroling His nativity
　　　His life imparts
immortality
　　　His whole and part
are our Heaven within.

Heralding His felicity
　　　that thrills our hearts
in humble receptivity
　　　whose perfect art
is Heaven within.

In our silence
　　　His glory chimes
as complete science
　　　parable and rhyme
of Heaven within.

In tender reliance
　　　we transcend time
and gain alliance
　　　with His sublime
Heaven within.

Reaching the Goal
Holland, January 1995

As I reach the supreme goal of existence
melting rivers rush without resistance
through the terrain of my universe
as the rhythms of cosmic verse.

Undulating rivers rise as fountains
spraying their showers like snow-capped mountains
melting into spring's waterfalls,
descending into my Self heavenly enthralled.

Rising through my Being the rivers climb
flowing through each cell in delicate chime
thrilling me in extremes of ecstasy
as they weave together Self's frequencies

of shimmering silence in tenderest motion
touching the core of sweetest emotion.
The rivers swell as God's love in me
enveloping me with His Divinity.

Earth in the Balance

Livingston Manor, January 1993

O Mother Earth,
    your sacredness sings in the orbiting moon
whose luster cascades into our souls.
    Your divinity dances in the swelling waves
ever settling back in the ocean's whole.
    Your Heaven hums in the hovering sky
whose ceiling is our own infinity.
    Your blessedness beams in the breathtaking sunrise
whose daily birth reveals life's ubiquity.

O Mother Earth,
    your wind gave us our first breath
made sweet by the meadow flowers.
    Your vibrant air sustains all life
with the vital force of God's power.
    Your rivers run through our very veins
rushing with undiluted purity.
    Your stars light the ethereal heavens
pulsating as our hearts' peaceful maturity.

O Mother Earth,
    we can belong to your land
but you cannot be subdued by man
    for you are the cosmic web of life
and we exist only as a strand.

Yet in each delicate fiber
lies the entire universe—
  the whole within each part interlaced—
an intelligent sheet of harmonious verse.

O Mother Earth,
  if we don't protect your precious soil
mountains, forests, rivers, lakes
  then we are harming our own thread
in the divine tapestry of God's make.
  May our every step be respectful—
to every pine needle, the balmy breeze,
  the soft mist and every grain of sand,
gentle waterfalls and the fruit-bearing trees.

O Mother Earth,
  let man and Nature again unite
for imbalanced, our livelihood is destroyed.
  Balanced, you rain your nourishment
fertilizing our being with Nature's joys.
  We inherit your balance in the Unified Field—
the home of Natural Law within consciousness.
  Transcending to our own Self-referral silence
our acts become aligned with Nature's righteousness.

O Mother Earth,
    Man and Nature regain their balance
when man returns to his own nature within
    where his Being unites with the universe—
life's joyous wheel in eternal spin.
    Earth rejoicing in the balance
heralds Heaven's glorious descent
    sliding from the sky on a soft rainbow
bathing the globe with divine merriment.

Shimmering
Holland, October 1992

Shimmering darkness
shimmering space
shimmering wholeness
of each point encased
in shimmering circles
opening into waves
of spiraling particles
in my silent enclave.
Shimmering you come
in a stirring rush
awakening the hum
of the shimmering hush.
Shimmering you rain
shimmering you flow
filling my domain
with your glistening glow
like thousands of suns
and the shining moon
upon the rippling ocean
of my liquid cocoon.
Shimmering darkness simmering still
showering you ever reappear
spreading sweetest blissful thrills
shimmering crystal clear.

The Prairie's Government

(in honor of the Natural Law Party, and inspired by
Walt Whitman's vision of a new, more universal government
to be established soon in the fair prairie fields.)
Holland, July 1992

In the airy place
    of the prairie's golden face
the worn wrinkles of time
    vanish in the open space
of timelessness.

Without the prairie, life ages
    as history's long pages
binding eternity
    to the world that stages
illusion's charming caress.

But the prairie serves to remind
    of Being's eternal straight line
fanning in all directions
    without hills to bind
its calming ubiquitousness.

In the prairie, one feels
    the silent Self unseals
into the fields' expanse
    which no longer conceals
the plains of unboundedness.

The prairie bestows the power
    of silence that unseen, showers
the seeds of Natural Law
    like yeast hiding in flour
in its all-pervasiveness.

The prairie yearly yields
    all crops from one fair field
of all possibilities
    whose power lovingly wields
the grains of blessedness.

The prairie is tranquility
    yet dynamic in ability
to give endless abundance
    from soil of fertility
providing wholesomeness.

Standing royal and grand
    on the pious prairie's land—
Nature's Government—
    whose Laws man can command
from within consciousness.

To its Self, the prairie confides
    Nature's laws inside—
a constitutional blueprint
    that for man and nation guides
back to peacefulness.

As the prairie reaches
        to the sky, it beseeches
us to return to the land
        whose silent stretch teaches
Nature's resourcefulness.

Embedded in the prairie's earth
        is the Constitution of the Universe—
the rule of Natural Law
        that alone gives birth
to sovereign righteousness.

Kingdom of Heaven
Holland, July 1992

I desire your Grace.
You come to me
as rivers race
to a motionless sea—
luminous beams
of waltzing light
that close the seams
of the dark night.
I knock on your door
and turn the key;
I enter your core
of silent luxury—
a gilded vestibule
of soft symmetry
encrusted with jewels
affording felicity—
a palatial home
of regal splendor,
a sacred dome
of self surrender.
I climb the stairs
that spiral
into the glare
of mirrored aisles
that Self-reflect
Self's vision

and re-project
Self's cognition.
I open the window
to sky's ornament—
a soft rainbow
of Heaven's descent.
Touching both ends
of the universe
infinity bends
Heaven to Earth.
I call Your Grace.
You sweetly come
as shimmering lace—
Heaven's kingdom.
The royal decree
your whisper imparts:
to love God always
with all one's heart.

Self, the Temple
Holland, July 1992

The Sabbath has come.
The bells are chiming.
Are not all days holy?
Is not Self the temple—
Heaven of the midday sun?

It is time for scripture,
To offer prayer.
Is not silence the sermon?
Is not bliss the lord
In one's Self ever secured?

The choir is singing,
The organ-master playing.
Are not the birds as joyful,
The wind as melodious?
Is not God everywhere ringing?

All are coming to hear,
To be redeemed.
Is not silence the soft sound
Where one is reborn in eternity
Attaining oneness intimately dear?

God speaks in silence—
Altar of the heart.
Is not one's Being divine—
The shrine of pure love—
Surrendering to which one gains alliance?

America

Holland, June 1992

America, America
from sea to shining sea
Thy glory ever reigns—
majestic, mountainous beauty
vast, amber plains
dynamic, rushing rivers
placid, crystal lakes
bounteous wealth-giver
God-given for mankind's sake.

America, America
Thy founding fathers decreed
alliance with the rule of Natural Law
rendering all men free
to enjoy life without flaw
to pursue happiness, liberty
as humankind's inalicnable right
to fulfill governmental authority
to lift life to this sacred height.

America, America
all cultures melt in Thee
as the ocean absorbs each wave
land of the free,
home of the brave
where diversity breathes togetherness

crowned by desire for good.
Americans are blessed
intent on brotherhood.

America, America
return to Thy Constitution
that governs the universe
which alone can bring fruition
to Heaven on our dear earth.
Let Natural Law be Thy guide—
perfection of Nature's government
where one party rule abides
leading mankind to fulfillment.

America, America
let dawn's early light
shine in every heart
where men stand proud to fight
with wisdom that imparts
peace which in twilight gleams
star-spangled across the sky
fulfilling the American Dream—
justice solemnized.

America, America
Thy duty embraces nations
to protect with nourishing peace
then enmity in world relations
will finally cease.

All cold wars will quickly thaw
as each nation finds the key
to the rule of Natural Law
whereby God sheds His grace on Thee
and on all nations eternally.

Divine Artist

Holland, January 1992

His soft brush
strokes silence into form.
From his hush
appears the Absolute unborn.
As rivers rush
his vibrant hues take vision.
Delicately lush
they manifest his inner cognitions.
Like the evening thrush
creating melody
yet more plush
inspiring rhapsody;
as darkness is crushed
with dawning rays
his paintings flush
as bliss portrayed.
As water-springs gush
he unleashes his designs
bowing with sublime blush
purest channel of the Divine.

Finest Feeling
Holland, January 1992

More powerful than word is feeling
softly revealing
the flow of silence's ocean.
Feeling is the language of the heart
that imparts
the depths of tenderest emotion.

Silence is the heart of the Divine
that binds
all men in love's freedom.
In purity of heart, feelings convey
in their sway
the message of God's Kingdom.

Just a mother's warm smile
to child
says more than sweetest phrase.
Mother's feeling is all-knowing,
flowing
to child in kind tacit praise.

Feelings transmit as waves of sound
that unseen, bound
and rebound throughout creation.

Feelings pass over land to farthest place
in instant pace
all distance neared in love's infinite correlation.

Never hurt one's finest feeling
tightly sealing
love's unrestricted streams.
An open heart flowing free as a dove
with love
touches all with warmth of the Supreme.

To one's feelings always give nourishment
with intent
of respectful appreciation.
All tender feelings are rays of God's will
which in resonance thrill
the universe with His jubilation.

Constitution of the Universe

Holland, January 1992

Entering a zone
where time stands still
through a light cone
into silence filled
with thousands of grains
of vibrating frequencies—
a coherent plane
of crystal transparency.
This silence is charioteer
leading without flaw
as each impulse adheres
to the command of Natural Law
that governs both galaxy
and tiny atom
with effortless intricacy
within the Self fathomed
as the Constitution
of the Universe
bringing to fruition
Heaven on the earth.
The structure of the cosmos
connects life in its alliance,
links the opposed—
dynamism and silence,
point with whole,
seed with tree,

man with his soul,
unity and diversity.
In the transcendental field
of Self-cognition
each spiral is sealed
as Nature's inscription
bringing revelation
of God's Word—
Heaven's elation—
through turning inward.
This universal constitution
reigns unseen
guiding man's evolution
to unite with the Supreme.

Self's Resplendence
Holland, January 1992

O Sun, Thy brilliance surpasses the extremes
of the universe
touching every point with undulating beams
in rhythmic verse
of dancing light.

Quelling all darkness with Thy flames
that utter
the sound of its sparks, yet tames
silence that flutters
like a bird in flight.

Pouring oblations into this conflagration
kindles its fire
which never burns—only blinds in illumination
like bejewelled attire
adorning the night.

Consuming all life in Thy glorious blaze
into blissful peace
then igniting into an all-seeing gaze
which again decreases
like sun at twilight.

In simplicity Thy radiance comes.
Bathing in Thy glow
of shimmering, sweet softness is Heaven won
in an embryo
of celestial delight.

O Sun, to bask in Thine incandescence—
Thy lustrous paradise—
is to know life's pure, inner resplendence:
one's Self cognized
in Thy sacred sight.

Full Moon Night

Holland, July 1991

Full moon light spread throughout the sky
opposing darkness with softest light,
beneath your gentle coolness all life lies
basking in the fullness of your sacred sight.

Going beyond the stars into your silent whole—
ever captivating in its misty glow—
lighting the essence of all tender souls
as your absoluteness one comes to know.

Your force stirs winds, changes tides
eternally looping back to fully waxed state.
Without effort from point to fullness you ride
as Natural Law itself, unseen, pulsates.

Swinging with you in opposite extremes
in lulling rhythms creates Self's frequencies.
Self slips back along your beams
into wholeness, your serene unity.

Royally you sit between sky and earth—
Heaven itself lighting both ends.
Yet within you is the entire universe—
all life is encompassed in your lustrous bend.

All hearts are drawn to your magnitude—
your luster that inspires holiness—
churning devotion into a humbling mood
which melts into oneness—life's sweetest quest.

Supreme Love

Holland, March 1991

My love is touching all creation
with warmth of tenderest feelings
returning to Self in Self-adoration
lover and loved congealing
into oneness, then spreading apart
for love to always flow
as streams from a melted heart
where knower loves to know
Self as untainted love itself
for Self is love divine.
Supreme love in silence dwells
knower and known entwined.
Lover, loving, loved merged in lovingness
know deepest intimacy
where one is the other in tender Beingness
ever united in ecstasy.
In unity, trinity sweetly conceives
love true and pure.
No need to give or receive
in eternal love secured;
then love loves for loving's sake
as a flower that blooms.
Flowing endlessly as river to lake
Self-love is never consumed.

To love one's Self is to love everything—
all life sweetly embraced.
Self-sufficient and free I sing
overflowing in supreme love's grace.

The Waters of Life

Holland, January 1991

The rivers are rising today
rushing in rapid force
coming from all directions
to joyfully unite with their source.

The ocean welcomes each stream
absorbing them into her whole
as they churn the silent depths
to swell into gentle rolls.

The rivers are slowing down
opening into a crystal lake
stirring fluorescent bubbles
as they spread their foamy wake.

The lake is becoming still
as each ripple vanishes from sight—
only myself in reflection
surrounded by the sun's shimmering light.

I'm entranced in the river's dance
from sea to lake to sea;
life's river is unity's curve
flowing from me, back to me—all within me.

The rivers, ocean, and lake
appear as separate notions
but all are waves of myself
sweetly moving in different motions.

The Sacred Land

Holland, October 1990

Stepping onto the sacred land
Bowing to touch
The soft sacred dust
From which springs all creation

Breathing the sacred breath—
The sacred air
Here, there, and everywhere
Which gives rise to all creation

Hearing the sacred sound—
The sacred hum
As life's continuum
In eternal reverberation

Seeing the sacred light—
The sacred form
Of each impulse gently born
From silence forming into creation

Drinking the sacred sea—
The sacred waters
Flowing to all quarters
In spiraling transformations

Coming to the sacred place—
My sacred home—
My Self alone
In breathless adoration

Mount Shiva

Switzerland, June 1990

Each day I gaze upon Thy sacred form
rising from the water, coning up to the sky.
Every moment a new face is born—
from dusty sunset to the rosy sunrise.

Thy golden snow-capped peak ablaze
disappears into cotton puffs of white
then translucently covered in misty haze
appears again silent in the full moonlight.

The twinkling stars adorn Thy crown
lighting the firmament.
Glittering snow particles bejewel Thy gown
casting the light of Heaven's descent.

O mightiest of mountains deserving of fame
ruling royally from above the clouds
immovable, unshakeable is Thy reign
noble, humble, yet mysteriously proud!

Thy sacredness is in Thy rarest power
to inspire unending, overwhelming awe.
God's full glory Thou dost forever shower
humbling all to Thy heavenly call.

See Only the Light

Switzerland, March 1990

Wherever there is darkness there is also light
always shining, even on darkest of days.
Putting your attention on the light
the light will grow
until the darkness is completely erased.

Look for the light that always shines
behind every cloud, within every soul.
The power of attention can transform your life
making you whole
by favoring the light that everywhere glows.

To dwell on the thorn, or delight in the rose—
the choice is there in every situation.
Choose to keep your attention on the light
and your life will flow
in the beauty of God's creation.

Evening Silence

Switzerland, April 1990

My silence is spilling into the evening air
pouring onto the ground, reaching the skies
here, there, and everywhere.
Where am I
as I lose my individuality
to this silent sea overtaking me?
I stand in breathless adoration
caught in fascination
as my silence unfurls
into each world—
the universe of each textured leaf
the canyons in the bark of every tree
the rosy, pink clouds crowning the snow-capped peaks
fanning across the misty sky in gentle, dusty streaks.
Every cell of my being is rejoicing in the pristine freshness
thrilled with each step I take.
I'm no longer immured by my physiology
which is as porous as the air around me.
All of Nature is conversing with me—
the soft humming breezes
the rustling leaves.
The sweet scent of hyacinth is calling me near
even the pulsating, vibrant air I hear.

The sinking sun is now saying "good night"
as she puts all Nature to rest
in the heavenly silence of the glittery dusk
until the dawning light.

Thy Thousand Eyes

Switzerland, March 1990

Thine eyes reflect Thy silence within Thy whole
always gazing in upon their Self, they know
reality.
Nothing can escape their penetrating vision
for they are all-seeing, with absolute precision—
Totality. .
Sparkling like sapphires casting blue luster,
twinkling as stars in arrayed clusters
they blind like lightning with their brilliance.
Their expanding pupils bestow peaceful darkness of night.
They forever flutter like the wings of a new bird in flight.
They not only see but
hear
touch
taste
smell
and feel.
All senses, connected like fingers meeting at the palm of the ha
reveal
one consciousness in motion—all knowingness congealed.
O, the splendor of Thine eyes
staring at me
draws me into their hypnotic power.
As they open and close, I become entranced
in the universe revealed in every vibrant glance
and in the silence I see beyond their lens of transparency.

Viewing their beauteous perfection
I see them watching me in wakeful attention
but they are just delighting in seeing their own Self.

Caught

Switzerland, March 1990

Becoming unbound
Cutting asunder the knots of matter
Escaping boundaries
Emancipated from relative fetters

Finally free
From all binding connections
Moving unhindered
In prisms of omni-direction

No longer immured
All restrictions joyously released
Only to be captured
In the bliss of Thy heavenly peace

Mother Divine

Switzerland, February 1990

The breath of Mother Divine is the breath of Nature
in softness aligned.
Her slightest exhalation moves the entire cosmos.
Every speck of intelligence
in readiness stands in obeisance to her tender command.
By governing her Self—Nature's Government Divine—
the tendrils of her love transform the trends of time.

Her Heaven she reflects to all life in vibrant precision
mirroring back again and again, making more whole
each point of Heaven in expanded bliss. Thus her role—
bringing Heaven's descent—fulfilling God's mission
to open all eyes to their own heavenly vision.

Heaven
Switzerland, February 1990

Heaven is dancing before my eyes
vibrant in every particle of creation;
Heaven is my silence cognized
spurred into tenderest fluctuation.
Heaven I see alive in every flower,
the soft sky, the trees swaying in the wind;
Heaven is my sparkling Self empowered
folding silently deeper and deeper within.
Heaven I see descending in waterfalls,
bubbling in brooks, shimmering on streams;
Heaven is my Self divinely enthralled
interlaced in a thousand luminous beams.
Heaven I see glittering in the twilight,
smiling on the moon, pulsating in the stars;
Heaven is my brilliant white light
lighting the universe near and far.
Heaven I see in dusty pastel sunsets,
angel-hair clouds, and the dawning of day.
Heaven is my Self casting its net
enveloping all in luminescent rays.
Heaven I see aglow in mountain-touched skies
sweeping into grassy valleys below.
Heaven is my inner wakeful paradise
in perception reflected as bliss superimposed.

Sweet Spring
Switzerland, February 1990

Spring, spring, sweet spring is coming;
the tingling air is alive and humming.
Life is being reborn,
the trees and meadows adorned
with spring, spring, sweet spring.

Spring, spring, sweet spring is approaching near
as the first pastel blossoms magically appear.
Each seed swells in fullness
tenderly from within emptiness
into spring, spring, sweet spring.

In spring, sweet spring, life begins anew;
as silence awakens, each fiber warmly accrues
arousing from hibernation
each gentle germination
into spring, spring, sweet spring.

Spring, spring, sweet spring is circling around again.
Rose petals from Heaven softly descend.
God is bestowing His grace,
smiles light every face
rejoicing in spring, spring, sweet spring.

A Snowfall

Switzerland, January 1990

The sky is spilling its softness
as snowflakes drift slowly down. Upon the ground
the blessings of silence are received all around.
Nothing can disturb the wintry stillness—
the peace of God, the peace of bliss.
Yet in the distance, sweetly, I hear
a spark of life—the morning bird. She chirps and sings
the first awakening of the coming spring.
I ponder... as I sink into my own silent sphere
the beauty of this moment, this day, each season
year after year.

God's Voice Within You

Switzerland, January 1990

Listen to your innermost feelings
hear the whisper of God in you—
forever divinely appealing
His thoughts tenderly rising through you.

Listen to your own inner voice
steering your every direction;
fleeting notions and wavering choices
cease in silent wisdom's perfection.

In your heart He forever dwells
always there to support each need
gracefully concealed in the bottomless well
rising to guide every deed.

Act upon God's voice in you;
harmoniously flow in His song.
Every thought, word, and act will sing true
empowering you in right, and weakening all wrong.

Always go by your innermost feelings;
hold on tightly to God's leading hand.
Gain trust in His quiet revealings
and walk in the light of His Divine Plan.

Coming Home

Switzerland, December 1989

In the evening mist you are coming near
    closer, closer
My being wakes to hear

Your humming whispers echo through the air
    waiting, waiting
Each moment I can hardly bear

As you slowly turn silence's key
    pounding, pounding
My heart beats breathlessly

Upon entering, this home becomes alive
    thrilling, thrilling
My being now that you've arrived

O, to feel you home once more
    tenderly, tenderly
Like a bird my heart soars

In every room make yourself at home
    never, never
Again from this blessed house roam

Fill every chamber, alcove, and space
    fuller, fuller
Until every corner is divinely encased.

"No more vacancy," I want to ring
      louder, louder
"My house is fully occupied," I joyously sing

May this abode always be gracious and pure
      so forever, and ever
In this home your love will sweetly endure

Awake in the Full Moon Light

Switzerland, December 1989

I lie awake basking in the full moon light
absorbing her lustrous rays.
Yet I am awake every night;
my every night shines like the day
with thousands of moons casting their glow
waning and waxing to and fro.

I lie asleep yet awake within
absorbing the balmy breeze.
Every night I'm awake in the soft wind
with air currents blowing through me with ease
gathering force, sweeping away all notion
leaving liquid silence in whirlpooling motion.

I lie awake, hearing the whistling hum
hollowing through the air.
Every night I'm awake in the whirling strum
that vibrates in me and everywhere
absorbing the peaks of each tonal frequency
as they swell in pitch reverberating through me.

I lie awake entranced in stargazing
absorbing the silent space.
Every night I see all the stars blazing
veiling the twilight in shimmering lace
bursting like fireworks in myriad streams
nightly witnessed in my cosmic dreams.

I lie awake fathoming the universe
absorbed in Heaven's light.
In each sparkling point I see Heaven's birth—
in me Heaven forever resides—
the twinkling stars, whistling hum, radiant moon
are my own ever wakeful, heavenly cocoon.

The Enchanted Forest
Winter
Switzerland, December 1989

The frosty forest is a magical wonder today
as the sun lights up the silver-branched ceiling.
Everywhere I look I become caught in the beauty—
every tree is me
I am every tree—
one sparkling reality
where even time stands frozen
in the soft mist of unity.

The enchanted forest is alive and humming
as the fresh wind sets the snow falling
stirring all senses in the ethereal coolness.
Each beauteous illusion
stills all confusion
into a vaporous fusion
of frothy silence, pure as snow
where even a whisper is an intrusion.

Dancing and glistening are all hues of milky white—
snowflake crystals of perfect symmetry
blanket this celestial haven of wintry peace.
Angels appear
shimmering clear
caroling in cheer
the echoey song of this wondrous winterland:

"Peace, peace, heavenly peace, is here peace, heavenly peace."

Pour Thy Love

Switzerland, December 1989

Pour Thy love down upon me—
Let the sky open its rivers;
Fill me till I am overflowing
Most bounteous, Divine Giver.

Pour Thy love down upon me—
Let the Heavens spill their waterfalls;
Fill me till I am overflowing
In Thy waters deeply enthralled.

Pour Thy love down upon me—
Sliding down rainbow beams;
Fill me till I am overflowing
Immersed in Thy holy streams.

Pour Thy love down upon me—
Let Thy gates flood open upon me;
Fill me till I am overflowing
Submerged in Thy foamy sea.

Pour Thy love down upon me—
In waves of soothing motion;
Fill me till I am overflowing
Till Thy currents merge into one ocean.

My Sacred Tulsi

Switzerland, November 1989

Last night I had the sweetest dream
of the sojourn to my blessed home.
Upon arrival I opened my verandah screen
to see how splendid my garden had grown.
There she stood—radiant, full, and taciturn—
her smiling leaves bowing to greet me.
In welcome praise of my return
she immediately offered her nutriment humbly.
In the air our feelings entwined
as I looked to her and she up to me.
At that moment we were one in heart and mind—
my darling, dearest, Sacred Tulsi.

As I awoke my heart continued to spill in adoration
to this life-giving plant gracing my pathway.
What power she has, rousing such infatuation
even thousands and thousands of miles away!
Most revered of all plants and trees
sanctifying the air of holiest temples and shrines.
Through her, colorless sap flows with ease
full of bliss-healing nutrients of the Divine.
O how my heart ardently swells
longing for her nourishing vitality.
Is she being watered and taken care of well—
my darling, dearest, Sacred Tulsi?

More than Heaven—
Merging with the Transcendent
Switzerland, November 1989

I thought I knew what happiness was
always moving in surface content;
then in silence I met you—
a meeting of divine portent.
Daily I came to know you more
with sweetest fervent intent
till one day my heart poured open
as a waterfall in rapid descent.
Like a river succumbing to the ocean
was my last ripple of relent
as Thy tidal waves consumed me
ceasing all repent.
I melted into You, and You into me
all points merging in merriment
into a dark, throbbing, tinseled thickness
knowing no discernment.
Your spiraling particles You revealed to me
as one vibrating instrument—
each string uniting diversity to its source
as a coil inwardly bent.
Now I feel Your thrills undulate through me
in wavy filament
connecting all parts into a translucent shell
harboring the pulsating firmament.

As I envelop You, You envelop me
in perfect alignment;
this union's felicity is more joyous than Heaven
breathing tenderest fulfillment.

Victory

Switzerland, October 1989

Come fly with me in the endless sky
Beyond all clouds into ecstasy;
Come swing with me from star to star
As they burst into thousands of infinities.

Come soar with me in the porous space
Sprinkled with the windless spray;
Come leap with me onto the moon
As it wanes and waxes in tender sway.

Come coast with me on wave upon wave
As each bends into circular motion;
Come glide with me in the glistening glow
Of a silent substance in the foamy ocean.

Come drift with me—never aimlessly
On the rapid river's melting rush;
Come sail with me upon the shimmering sheet
In the soundless static, the humming hush.

Come swim with me in the milky waters
Sweetly submerging again and again;
Come climb with me to that highest peak
Beyond which is no beginning or end.

Come float with me in the glittery night
Where darkness is effaced by the brilliant sun;
Come dive with me into the spiraling heavens
And emerge victorious in Totality won.

The Sights and Sounds of Seelisberg
Switzerland, August 1989

A shimmering silver sheet
dances before my eyes
as the sun reflects your rippling stillness.
The majestic mountains boldly rise from your waters
to royally grace the skies.
A view so breathtaking—is it real
or just a wondrous illusion
God has magically revealed?

The soft, fresh rain
unleashes every shade of green
and vibrant aromas of sweetest pine
enhance every breath of my Being
gracing my sight and the space between
with a textured stillness. Is this life itself—
or just a bewitching moment,
a reflection of my Self?

The vast grassy meadows
canopied with colorful wildflowers
set the spirit to run swift and free
up that one path where the pointed peak is the goal
and the sun thaws the snow into blissful showers
of bubbling streams and suspended waterfalls
that enrapture me to swoon and swirl.
Is this the song the valley calls?

This haven of Heaven
sacredly perched above the clouds
beckons the world with its call
of silence and beauty within and without
echoing from peak to peak, full and loud.
Can you hear the Alpine horn's beseeching wish—
peace from the level of peace itself—
the truth, men for generations have missed?

The Enchanted Forest
Summer
Switzerland, October 1989

What does the magic forest speak to me?
A whisper I hear beneath its pine ceiling stillness—
Every bark, every cone telling its own story,
Worlds within worlds revealing their glory.

The sparkling sun filters through the rustling needles
Refracting her rays, diffusing her glow,
Lighting the silence in golden greens,
Awakening the vibrancy so alive yet serene.

The fragrance of pine perfumes the air
Sweetly rousing every cell of my Being
To its own intelligent, lively felicity
So pure, so fresh—the breath of settled simplicity.

This forest enchantingly tells many tales
Of illusion, of reality—Nature's ever-changing stage—
With a cast of birds merrily singing every role,
Each leaf and bark acting its part to narrate the whole.

Am I the Poet?

Switzerland, July 1989

Am I the poet of this poem
of each expression rising from within?
Silence stirred, an impulse heard
beyond all meter, beyond all word . . .

Am I the writer of these lines
of each phrase appearing on my screen?
A seed sown for silence to flow
in any wave the wind blows . . .

Am I the composer of this song
of the sounds of silence singing?
Wholeness bent on self-intent
for me to be silence's instrument . . .

Can I claim popular authorship
when I am just a joyous witness
of each lyrical notion in the swelling ocean
of pure silence in tender motion?

Music

Switzerland, July 1989

Music awakens the soul
to find one's God
in that field where silence sings.
Music melts one's heart
to warmly open to God
in that hum from where primordial sound springs.

Music lifts one's emotions
to the heights of divinity
in that Heaven of cosmic harmony.
Music fills one's Being
in fullness of God's love
for love is God's symphony.

Music is pure life flowing
in self-referral melodies—
wholeness swinging in infinite frequencies.
Music is God
vibrant in every form—
my divine music singing within me.

Song of the Morn
India, March 1989

"Awake, awake
to this sparkling morning,"
the multitude of birds are warmly calling.

"Arise, arise,
the sun is dawning,"
the bees and butterflies are gently humming.

"Hark, hark,"
the birds in chorus chirp away,
"forever new is each precious day."

"Rejoice, rejoice,"
the flowers are singing,
"in the sweeetness of your blossomed
Being."

"Breathe, breathe,"
the leaves whisper everywhere,
"the life breath of the fresh morning air."

"Live, live,"
the trees laugh heartily,
"the awakened vibrancy of your Totality."

"Celebrate, celebrate,"
is the song of the morn.
"Each moment anew is wholeness reborn."

He is My Lord
India, February 1989

He who laughs in the form of flowers
who smiles in the twinkling of the stars
whose song is in the rustling wind
whose eternity is in every hour...

He whose whole is in every grain of sand
whose heart flows as rushing streams
whose radiance is the cool full moon
whose love is the essence of man...

He whose warmth is in the dawning morn
whose softness is misty raindrops
whose light is the rays of the sun
whose infinity is every moment born...

He whose greatness is the vast universe
whose gentleness is in the falling snow
whose joy is the singing birds
whose grace is Heaven on Earth...

He whose silence is the depth of the ocean
whose peace is in the clear blue sky
whose bliss is in bubbling brooks
He is my Lord, my Self, my Silence in motion.

Mother Ganga
India, February 1989

Thy sight stills me into serenity
Sinking me into the depths of my Being.
Thy refreshing air washes away all weariness
Awakening me in the softness of my Totality.

Submerged in Thy silent flow
Thy power restores me to my Self.
Thy ripples of infinity seep through me
With the peace Thou dost endlessly bestow.

In Thy waters I am never again the same
With Thy currents rushing through me
Swiftly rinsing away all impurity
Bathing me in the wholeness of my sovereign domain.

As the setting sun paints Thee with her golden rays
The first smiling stars sparkle in Thy holy waters.
A cool breeze gently brushes upon my face—
O Mother Ganga, in fullness, I sing Thy praise!

Divine Mother

India, December 1988

Is She an illusion or is She real—
So sublimely ethereal
Appearing solid yet surreal?

Is She pure silence or is She motion
Or just a faint and joyous notion?
Is She Heaven or is She earth
Embracing the entire universe?

Is She star-laced nights
Or the moon's glowing light—
Expressing our vision's sweetest delight?

Is She tenderness or is She powerful—
She who is invincible in gentleness?
Is She laughter or bubbling bliss
Enveloping all in wholeness?

Is She creation's diversity
Or is She life's unity
Binding all differences in harmony?

She is all this, and even more—
She is the essence of what we live for.
She is in you, She is in me
Shining forever divinely.

Here and Now
India, Fall 1988

All that exists is here and now
The past never was, the future never will be
Only at this moment is my reality.

Only my reality exists here and now
Your reality is non-existent for me
For I am all that there is, that ever will be.

Each moment of my here and now
Is a flowing continuum of eternity—
My Self ever-present as lively unity.

Live well each moment of here and now
Revel in creation's beauty.
Encapsuled in each moment of here and now
is God's Divinity.

Power of Peace
India, Summer 1988

What is that power that destroys
bestowing supremacy?
Every nation's racing to employ
this greatest of fallacies.

What is that power where might is right
declaring victory?
Is this power when death cries in the night
throughout our history?

What is that power of knowledge incomplete
creating dangerous rivalry,
causing fear in never-ending defeat
by ignoring Nature's Totality?

What is that power where life is suppressed
with every nation in "courageous" conquest?
This is the power of the powerless
creating a world of peaceless unrest.

What is that power which continually creates
from within the unmanifest
a dynamic field that silently generates
coherence in world consciousness?

What is that power where right is might
giving every nation sovereignty?
It's the power of pure knowledge, life's pure light
revealed in Nature's Unity.

This is that power of invincibility
which every nation can gloriously own.
It's the power of harmony amidst diversity—
the Laws of Nature's home.

This power prevents the birth of an enemy;
it's the power of the truly powerful
whose strength lies in unity
for real power is always peaceful.

A Cosmic Ride
India, Summer 1988

The evening twilight is beckoning me
I hear in the rustling breeze,
"Come soar in cosmic ecstasy
Through the entire galaxy!"

Ascending in my aerial car
To traverse the firmament
I spiral down to the pole star
So near, yet seemingly distant.

Circumambulating this silent entity
The universe without commotion
I see stillness spreading to infinity
In threads of undulating motion.

Moving through the gentle, airy spray
A sudden explosion bursts asunder—
Stellar patterns in bountiful array
Disappear again into a void of wonder.

Collapsing into a dark vacuum of space
I am pulled by an invisible force
Where even light is completely effaced
Beyond the event-horizon's magnetic source.

Spinning into this curvature of space-time
Bent upon its own condensation
As a coiled string begins to unwind
A new universe I see in creation.

At this spherical boundary of the black hole
I navigate in opposite direction
Regaining sight of the universal whole
Avoiding total dissolution.

Entering into the Milky Way
A stretch of electronic points appear
In fiery brilliance shining like day
In diffusion sparkling clear.

Orbiting around the coolness of the moon
In fullness ablaze this night
I'm sprinkled by space dust everywhere strewn
Affording celestial delight.

Comets zoom past at lightning rates
Leaving translucent trails.
Spreading across the heavens in veil
The stars breathlessly pulsate.

The smiling sun with his supple beams
Blinds my delighted vision;
Thousands of transparent melting streams
Surround me and in softness glisten.

In him all power is compactly stored
Bubbling in inexhaustible energy—
The center of all planets sublimely adored
As the home of their radiant synergy.

Descending gently I greet the morn
Refreshed by expanded exaltation—
The Unified Field galactically adorned
Within me in illumination.

A Moment of Eternity
India, Summer 1988

Caught in a moment of eternity
Past and future in ever-present unity
Always the same, forever unchanged
In the gaps between every infinity

Caught in the web of time beyond all space
Silence spun perfectly in place
Always still, forever Thy will
One without a second, without a trace

Caught in the bliss of my Totality
Life's routine is seen as superimposed reality
Ecstatically glued, sweetly amused
Caught in my moment of eternity

Universal Mother

Switzerland, 1983

Higher than the highest
The essence of all
The nature of bliss
She's worshipped by all.
She shines like the moon
In radiant splendor;
White as pure crystal—
In her is life eternal.

Lovely as the lotus
Sweet as nectar pure
Beauty of the moon
She sings life's flowing tune.
Mother of Heaven
Mother of the Earth
Brilliant as the sun
She shines deep within everyone.

In My Happiness

Switzerland, January 1978

In my happiness
Thy love dwells;
In my openness
Thy love dwells;
In my fullness
Thy Self swells;
In Thy Being
I rest well;
In Thy giving
My heart swells;
In Thy Being
My heart dwells.

Thy Self

Switzerland, 1977

May my heart be full with Thee,
    full of Thy Self.
May my being flow to Thee,
    my self to Thy Self.
May my mind be deep in Thee,
    my self in Thy Self.
May my life reflect Thee,
    mirroring Thy Self.
May my thoughts be with Thee,
    only of Thy Self.
May my words speak Thee,
    Thy Self, nothing else.
May my joy express Thee,
    Thy unbounded wealth.
May my love forever love Thee,
    Thy Self, forever Thy Self.

Wintry Stillness
Switzerland, February 1975

A wintry feeling melts into one's vision
as a blanket of snow covers all life
in temporary hibernation.
The soft mist stands suspended
blessing me in momentary solitude.
Gentle snowflakes vanish into the gray lake.
All is still except the silent falling of the snow.

Devotion

Holland, June 2006

Devotion fills my heart.
Gratitude encompasses my soul.
These feelings are impossible to impart
without sacrificing the delicate whole.

In the bottom of the ocean
where silence is most deep
my heart revels in swelling emotions—
these tenderest feelings here I'll keep.

Only in the water's depths can they swell.
At the surface they are a tiny stream.
Let them rise and stay in this endless well
where truest love is redeemed.

Inexpressible is purest gratitude,
except by stillness's song.
Devotion is supreme beautitude
that in silence loudly belongs.

All

poems

are inspired

by the teachings of

His Holiness Maharishi Mahesh Yogi

and by experiences resulting from the practice of

the Transcendental Meditation® technique and

Transcendental Meditation Sidhi Program℠

and the beauty of nature.

Connect

I would love to hear from you!

Please contact me online at:

www.enlightenmentforeveryone.com/contact

Read about enlightenment, health,
world peace, and more at:

www.enlightenmentforeveryone.com/blog

www.huffingtonpost.com/ann-purcell

Facebook: www.facebook.com/Enlightenmentforeveryone

Twitter:

http://twitter.com/purcell_ann

About the Author

Ann Purcell has been a full-time teacher of Transcendental Meditation since 1973, teaching Transcendental Meditation and advanced courses in many countries around the world. She has also worked on curricula and course development for universities and continuing education programs.

She has been writing poetry and composing songs since 1975, in many beautiful locations during her travels around the world.

Ann Purcell is author of the award-winning book
*The Transcendental Meditation Technique
and the Journey of Enlightenment.*

Her most recent release is "You're a Hero"
a CD of songs for children.

She is also a regular contributor to the Huffington Post.

65550595R00136

Made in the USA
Charleston, SC
22 December 2016